Our Amazing States™

Arkansas
The Natural State

Miriam Coleman

PowerKiDS
press
New York

Published in 2011 by The Rosen Publishing Group, Inc.
29 East 21st Street, New York, NY 10010

First Edition

Editor: Joanne Randolph
Book Design: Greg Tucker
Layout Design: Kate Laczynski
Photo Researcher: Jessica Gerweck

Photo Credits: Cover, p 1 Ryan Beyer/Getty Images; p. 5 James Randklev/Getty Images; p. 7 MPI/ Hulton Archive/Getty Images; p. 9 © www.istockphoto.com/Nancy Nehring; p. 11 © Tom Till/age fotostock; p. 13 Jeremy Woodhouse/Getty Images; p. 15 © Bill Barksdale/age fotostock; pp. 17 (main image), 19, 22 (tree, bird, and flower) Shutterstock.com; p. 17 (inset) Joel Sartore/Getty Images; p. 22 (animal) © www.istockphoto.com/Nathan Hager; p. 22 (Douglas MacArthur) Hulton Archive/Stringer/ Getty Images; p. 22 (Johnny Cash) Michael Ochs Archives/Getty Images; p. 22 (William Clinton) Bruce Glikas/Getty Images.

Library of Congress Cataloging-in-Publication Data

Coleman, Miriam.
  Arkansas : the Natural State / Miriam Coleman. — 1st ed.
     p. cm. — (Our amazing states)
  Includes index.
  ISBN 978-1-4488-0655-3 (library binding) — ISBN 978-1-4488-0742-0 (pbk.) — ISBN 978-1-4488-0743-7 (6-pack)
  1. Arkansas—Juvenile literature. I. Title.
F411.3.C65 2011
  976.7—dc22

2009049518

Manufactured in the United States of America

CPSIA Compliance Information: Batch #WS10PK: For Further Information contact Rosen Publishing, New York, New York at 1-800-237-9932

Contents

The Natural State

Arkansas is nicknamed the Natural State for the beauty of its natural **landscape** and the plentiful wildlife living there. Arkansas is a land of mountains, **prairies**, waterfalls, caves, and forests. Flowers grow in a rainbow of colors and rivers run clear.

Arkansas is in the southern part of the United States. It was named after the Native American Quapaw tribe, which once lived there. Nearby Algonquin people called the Quapaw tribe the Arkansas, which means "south wind." Arkansas's flag has a diamond shape in its center, showing the gems that can be found in Arkansas's earth. It also has 25 stars, which show Arkansas's place as the twenty-fifth state in the **Union**.

This stream runs through Arkansas's Ouachita National Forest. It is in a part of the forest called Iron Springs.

From Territory to State

Arkansas was once part of a huge piece of land around the Mississippi River called the Louisiana Territory. This territory spread for more than 800,000 square miles (2 million sq km). The land had been claimed for France by a French **explorer** in the seventeenth century. In 1803, the United States bought this land from France with the Louisiana Purchase.

The United States soon split the land in two and named the northern part the Missouri Territory. The southern part became the state of Louisiana. In 1819, the United States split the northern part again and made the Arkansaw Territory. It was made up of present-day Arkansas and part of Oklahoma. On June 15, 1836, Arkansas became a state.

Here Spaniard Hernando de Soto and his followers discover the Mississippi River in 1541. They would go on to explore Arkansas, Oklahoma, and northern Texas.

History and Nature at the Arkansas Post

In 1686, Henri de Tonti opened a trading post at the Quapaw village of Osotouy, on the northern edge of the Gulf Coastal Plain. It was known as Poste de Arkansea. It was the first semipermanent French settlement in the lower Mississippi River valley. By 1819, the post was a busy port and the area's largest city. It was picked as the first capital of the Arkansas Territory.

Today the Arkansas Post is a national memorial. It has a museum where you can learn about the post's 300 years of history. Visitors can also explore trails through the site's prairies, forests, and marshes. The post is home to deer, turkeys, alligators, and many birds. The Arkansas Post is a great place to enjoy history and nature together!

American alligators, which were nearly gone from Arkansas, have made a comeback at the Arkansas Post. Today dozens of alligators live at the park.

From the Ozarks to the Mississippi

When people think of Arkansas, they often picture the Ozark Mountains. This forest-covered range is in northern Arkansas. Fast-moving streams cut through the mountains. The Ozark **Plateau** also spreads into Illinois, Missouri, and Oklahoma.

The Arkansas Valley, just south of the Ozarks, holds the Arkansas River. This is the state's largest river. Magazine Mountain, the highest point in the state, is there as well. Magazine Mountain is 2,753 feet (839 m) tall. The Ouachita Mountains spread from Oklahoma into the western side of Arkansas. The Mississippi River flows along Arkansas's eastern border. The river helps feed the rich soil of the nearby Arkansas Delta.

Hikers stand atop Hawksbill Crag, in the Ozark National Forest. Many people hike in the mountains and forest to enjoy nature up close.

Get Wild in the Natural State

Arkansas's wild places make great homes for many different animals. Black bears, bobcats, foxes, opossums, raccoons, skunks, and weasels are just a few of them. Arkansas is also home to many birds. Some of the birds found there are quail, ducks, wild turkeys, bluejays, cardinals, mockingbirds, and warblers. Arkansas's state animal is the fast-running white-tailed deer. It became the state animal in 1993.

About half of Arkansas's land is covered in forest. Ash, basswood, elm, maple, willow, oak, and pine trees all grow in the forests. Arkansas soil also grows many wildflowers, such as orchids, passionflowers, yellow jasmines, and wild verbenas.

The mockingbird became Arkansas's state bird in 1929. A mockingbird may learn up to 200 different songs in its lifetime.

Arkansas at Work

Factories in Arkansas make all kinds of food products. They also make metal parts for buildings, paper goods, tires, and electric **equipment**. Arkansas is the birthplace and headquarters of Wal-Mart, the biggest **discount** store chain in the country. It is home to two of America's biggest trucking companies as well. J.B. Hunt and Tyson Foods have their headquarters in Arkansas, too.

Arkansas farms raise livestock, or animals such as chickens, cows, and pigs, for food. They raise so many eggs and turkeys that they are one of the top producers of these goods in the country. Arkansas also grows crops such as cotton, soybeans, and wheat. It grows more rice than any other state.

A farmer watches as rice from his fields is poured into a grain truck. Arkansas has about 1.6 million acres (647,497 ha) of farmland being used to grow rice.

A Look at Little Rock

Little Rock is the capital of Arkansas and also its biggest city. Little Rock sits on a cliff above the Arkansas River. William Jefferson Clinton, the forty-second president of the United States, lived in Little Rock when he was governor of Arkansas. Today, you can learn all about the president at the William Jefferson Clinton Presidential Library. You can even step into a life-size model, or copy, of the Oval Office. At the Clinton library and museum visitors can also learn about what life is like in the White House.

If you want to find out what it is like to fly in outer space, you can do so at the Aerospace Education Center. You can take a peek inside a **flight simulator** there that is used to train real **pilots**!

Arkansas's state capitol has been the seat of its government since 1915. *Inset*: The Clinton Presidential Library has the largest holdings of any presidential library.

Hot Springs National Park

Arkansas is well known for its natural springs, or places where water rises up from under ground. Mammoth Spring is one of the largest natural springs in the nation. It pumps out 9 million gallons (34 million l) of water every hour.

At Arkansas's Hot Springs National Park, forces inside Earth heat the spring water. It can reach up to 143° F (62° C). Since early Native Americans lived in Arkansas, people have believed that bathing in Arkansas's spring water is good for your health. Starting in the nineteenth century, people built beautiful bathhouses, **health spas**, and hotels in Hot Springs. Hot Springs is also home to the Arkansas Alligator Farm and Petting Zoo!

Here you can see steam rising from the water in Hot Springs. *Inset*: There are many hotels and bathhouses near Hot Springs.

Visiting the Natural State

Even with all its wonderful wildlife, you still might not expect to find elephants in Arkansas. You can get close to these giant animals at Riddle's Elephant and Wildlife **Sanctuary** near Little Rock. The sanctuary takes in elephants that need a home. Often these elephants come from circuses and small zoos.

There are so many different things you can do in the Natural State. You can **canoe** on the Buffalo River or hike in the Ozarks. You can fish for trout in the White River or look for butterflies on Magazine Mountain. If you want to learn about history, you can visit Fort Smith, near the Ozark National Forest, or the Arkansas State University Museum, in Jonesboro. Arkansas has something for everyone!

canoe (kuh-NOO) To paddle through the water in a light, narrow boat that is pointed at both ends.

discount (DIS-kownt) Selling goods at a lower price.

equipment (uh-KWIP-mint) All the supplies needed to do an activity.

explorer (ik-SPLOR-er) A person who travels and looks for new land.

flight simulator (FLYT SIM-yuh-lay-tur) A machine that shows what it feels like to fly an aircraft.

health spas (HELTH SPAHZ) Places where people go to cure illness through hot springs and other treatments.

landscape (LAND-skayp) The landforms, such as hills, mountains, and valleys, in an area.

pilots (PY-luts) People who operate aircraft, spacecraft, or large boats.

plateau (pla-TOH) A broad, flat, high piece of land.

prairies (PRER-eez) Large, flat areas of land with grass but few or no trees.

sanctuary (SANK-choo-weh-ree) A place where people or animals are kept safe.

Union (YOON-yun) Another name for the United States that refers to the joining, or uniting, of the various states into one nation.

Arkansas State Symbols

State Tree
Pine Tree

State Animal
White-Tailed Deer

State Flag

State Bird
Mockingbird

State Flower
Apple Blossom

State Seal

Famous People from Arkansas

Douglas MacArthur
(1880–1964)
Born in Little Rock, AR
U.S. Army General

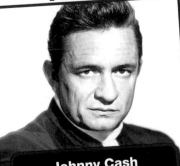

Johnny Cash
(1932–2003)
Born in Kingsland, AR
Country Musician

William Jefferson Clinton
(1946–)
Born in Hope, AR
U.S. President

Arkansas State Map

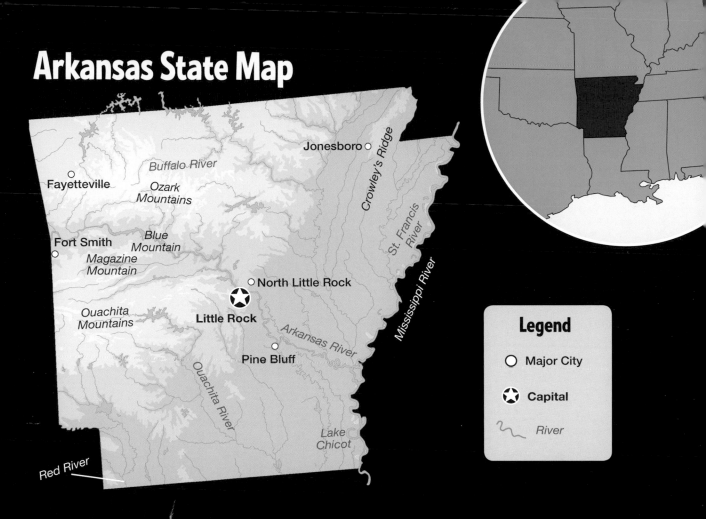

Jonesboro

Buffalo River

Fayetteville

Ozark
Mountains

Crowley's Ridge

Fort Smith

Blue
Mountain

St. Francis
River

Magazine
Mountain

North Little Rock

Mississippi River

Little Rock

Ouachita
Mountains

Arkansas River

Pine Bluff

Ouachita River

Lake
Chicot

Red River

Legend

○ Major City

⭐ Capital

〜 River

Arkansas State Facts

Population: About 2,779,154

Area: 53,183 square miles (137,743 sq km)

Motto: Regnat Populus ("The People Rule")

Song: "Oh, Arkansas," by Terry Rose and Gary Klaff

Index

Web Sites

Due to the changing nature of Internet links, PowerKids Press has developed an online list of Web sites related to the subject of this book. This site is updated regularly. Please use this link to access the list:

www.powerkidslinks.com/amst/ar/

4-11